Lincolnshire
COUNTY COUNCIL

discover libraries

**This book should be returned on or before
the due date.**

20 MAR 15
NCI 2/16

NC 3/18

To renew or order library books please telephone 01522 782010
or visit https://lincolnshire.spydus.co.uk
You will require a Personal Identification Number.
Ask any member of staff for this.

The above does not apply to Reader's Group Collection Stock.

D0269405

Travelling Tinker Man & Other Rhymes

Travelling Tinker Man & Other Rhymes

David Essex

Illustrations by Carlotta Christy

Contents

Foreword

Having written many lyrics for songs and shows, I thought
it would be an adventure to attempt to write a selection of
rhymes that captured moments in my life. I've called them
rhymes, as I thought to call them poems would be pretentious.

In *Travelling Tinker Man & Other Rhymes*, I write about
experiences of a charmed life, that may – I hope – resonate
with you, the reader. The subjects I write about encompass
music, family, fame and growing up in post-war England.

From flights of fancy, to situations I've lived through, here
are observations and thoughts from boyhood to manhood.
I hope that inside my thoughts and memories you will find the
spark of your own memories and perhaps you will give a smile
of recognition as you travel along the way.

David Essex OBE

Travelling Tinker Man & Other Rhymes

John Lennon

Strange to look back, how fate deals its hand,
I remember you mop head, in that world-changing band.
We covered your songs in a pub by the docks,
The locals would sing, the locals would rock.
I wanted Muddy Waters, but they wanted you,
The sound of the Sixties to help them get through.

She Loves You, Money, Twist and Shout,
Those covers we did would knock them all out.
I was blinkered and closed to the music you made,
Girls screaming and stuff when you hit the stage.
It ain't Memphis Slim, it's not Buddy Guy,
It was only your looks that made the girls sigh.
But you and your brothers, your brothers-in-arms,
Your songs and your voice would sound an alarm,
A bell that would ring with respect for you, John,
A respect for you, man, I admit I was wrong.
Your humour, your wit, your gift and your love,
Like Jesus, you said, a gift from above.

An honour to meet you that time in New York,
At the Grammy Awards, when we had our first talk,

When you told me Rock On was one of the best,
You thought it was special, stood out from the rest.
Those songs that you wrote, the songs that you sang,
Were part of my life, John, as a boy and a man.

Folk know where they were the day the King died.
I'm sorry, I don't and I don't think I cried.
But I remember the minute that you said goodbye,
I remember that moment and yes, I did cry.

Destiny

Fate, the child of destiny, where coincidence clashes
    with what might have been,
Crossroads with signposts, this way or that,
Fortune, charted by an enchanted black cat,
Which road left to follow and where will it lead?
Horoscope horrors, a rabbit's foot wish,
A shamrock discovered in the grey morning mist.
It's all in the book, it's all written down,
The twists and the turns, life's merry go round,
The circle of life, tomorrow's surprise,
Lies waiting and hidden away from our eyes.
Castles in the sand, journeys that reach
For distant horizons, with secrets to keep,
Shadows of past, turning the page with expectant fingers,
For tomorrow, today,
But patience and wait, don't wish life away.
Give thanks to your life for each breaking day.
A bump and a bruise will heal well in time
And black will turn golden when the planets align.
Walk the path carefully, gently with care,
For around every corner your fate's waiting there,
To carry you somewhere, to strangers unknown,

In future dark corners, to roll back the stone.
Then at the end, when destiny closes,
Look back and smile at your life's bed of roses.

A land fit for heroes

The guns, now silent, the moans of the near dead,
Like dark and pained whispers, fill up my head.
What is it for? Why are we here?
So far away in this hell of a place,
The smell, the mud, the fear on my face.

No tears left to cry, old before my time,
Me, a boy soldier, holding the line,
For King and for country, for England, for freedom,
For our way of life and our beautiful children,
For my people, my wife, so long since I've seen them.

I miss you, Dolly, I miss London town,
I hope you are safe as the bombs rain down,
Rain down and down on old London town.
We are doing our best, love, in this terrible war,
Doing our best on this strange foreign shore.
Keep safe now, my darling, and don't worry about me.

When this madness is over and England is free,
We will dance to the music, we will live life and then,
Catch up on lost time, all over again.

We will walk, gal, together, just us, hand in hand,
You and me, Dolly, and our little man.

How is he doing, is he missing his dad?
Please tell him I love him and not to be sad.
This can't last forever, one day, love, you'll see,
We will be together, you, David and me.
In your last letter, I remember you said,
You'd be leaving London for a much safer bed,
Evacuated somewhere, catching a train,
You wasn't sure where, though, a town with no name,
Somewhere better, safe, away from the Blitz,
Away from the madness, with the women and kids.

It's started again, the guns and the smoke,
But I've got my mates with me, a great bunch of blokes.
We will win this war, darling, I believe that we will,
When Jerry surrenders, when he's had his fill,
We'll return to old Blighty and one day I know,
I'll be home, back in England, in a land for heroes.

Mods and Rockers

Mods and Rockers, Tamla, Ska, Jerry Lee,
　　don't need a car,
Lambretta, Vespa and Bonneville, those
　　Brylcream boys remember still.
Southend, Brighton set the scene for
　　battles like you've never seen.
Fighting on the beaches there and fighting
　　in the town,
Rock the Mod, Mod the Rock, who will win
　　the crown?
Dirty greaser, poofy Mod, so, which tribe
　　were you?
Leather jacket, or anorak and Hush Puppy
　　shoes,
The girls would scream, the town would
　　shake as we stormed the beach.
Two armies from a different world, lessons
　　now to teach.

You're yesterday, you must be gay, two
　　tribes set to collide,

Battles won, we count the cost, as out of
town we ride.
Pink jeans torn, leather jackets ripped, Bank
Holiday seaside,
We did good, we won the day, they had
nowhere to hide.

Sorry about your holiday, but you see it had
to be done,
Cos they're not like us, they're a different
breed, under the Brighton sun.
The clothes they wear are really square,
born in the Fifties style,
Yeah, well look at you, Mr Fancy Pants, with
your pansy rank and file.
I'm an old-style Rocker, I'm a New Age Mod
and never the two shall meet,
A clash of style, a clash of look, we're
fighting in the street.

Those days have gone, it's for the best,
fashions ebb and flow.
What comes next I couldn't care less, as on
and on we go.

Now binge my drink, no need to think,
    legless Friday nights,
Idiots without a brain, just looking for a
    fight.
Girls like blokes stand and choke on the city
    centre street,
A and E just waits for me, they'll fix me up
    a treat.

Fairground attraction

Billy the Whizz, Jack the Dipper, hot dogs
    these dagoes, do you up like a kipper.
Little Richard, the lord of the ring, rattles the
    whip, with songs from the crypt,
Knuckledusters in a cluster, flick knives,
    greased-up Teddy Boys.
Roller coaster, win it for her, hit the target,
    cuddly toys.
Showmen, attractions, full of action, building
    nightmares, building dreams,
Screams of pleasure, hidden treasure, in a
    pirate's cove, by a ghostly train.
Spin my waltzer, bump my bumper, let me
    ride that ride again,
Teddy Boy, Teddy Girl, lost inside another
    world.
Noise and wonder, generator thunder, jive
    me, Teddy, make me twirl,
Roll on up, this ride is leaving, Hayley's comet,
    Bill's kiss curl.
Helter skelter, tell your fortune, let's all dance
    to a different tune,

Rock 'n' Roll me why not hold me,
underneath this gypsy moon?
Fairground attraction, full of action, here
tonight, but gone too soon.

The Royal Docks

I remember the docks, Dad took me to see the ships,

Just like buildings, sailing in from the sea,
The smell of the spices, the sweat of the men,
The Royal Docks was working, way back then.

From India and China, Australasia too,
With cargo aplenty for me and for you.
Stevedores, dockers, plundering cranes,
Ships from the world with wonderful names.

Banter, whistling, holds to unload
And on to the lorries and off down the road.
Strangers from strange lands, leaving the ship
And going to shore before the next trip.

Their colourful language and different face,
Men from the sea of every race,
Sheds full of cases of everything,
Imported and waiting, for country and King.

Flat caps on the stones waiting for work,
The lucky ones picked, the other ones hurt,
Brothers in dockland, mates to a man,
Doing their best, the best that they can.

This place was for men, this place was for muscle,
As I sat on Dad's shoulders in the hustle and bustle,
I wondered and thought of worlds far away,
Across tempest and storm, then the ships seem to say,
We ride out the storm and towering waves,
Steel mountains we are, no watery grave.

No SOS, no lost at sea,
We deliver our crew and dock safely.
The Royal Docks have gone now, the severance paid,
The dockers long gone, into that watery grave.

Theatre of dreams

Is there magic here, in these four walls?
Where actors have trod for history,
Where journeys have taken surprising turns,
Where moments are frozen in mystery.

Tears, laughter, comedy, the tragic,
The star and spear holder, the drama, the magic,
Still here in this room, this theatre of dreams,
A shrine to the arts and the changes of scene,
The opening, the closing, the tears of goodbye,
Shine just like diamonds in the past actor's eye.

There was once the poet, the King and the Queen,
The finest performance that you'd ever seen,
Bow upon bow, applause just like thunder,
Resonate in these walls and split them asunder,
With laughter and sighs, with truth and with lies,
The skeletons of the past, the original cast.

They were here for your pleasure, here for your joy,
Waiting for Godot, the Nutcracker's toys,
Costumes of fire, make up of gold,
Gone not forgotten, your torch I still hold.

The ghosts of your troubadours, the harlequins spin,
Matinee idols that made ladies' hearts sing.
Pantomime horses and men dressed as dames,
Clowns of the footlights cry out in pain.
Remember me, I was here, here before you,
I watch from the gods, I see what you do.
As you take to the stage in a glow of limelight,
Another adventure, another first night.

Looking back

What's your favourite colour, mate? Bill said to Ted.
Dunno, said Ted, could be blue, or it could be red.
I don't like yellow, mate, at all and orange, Bill, is horrible.
I saw an orange motor once, did that look bloody terrible.
Green is nice, restful and serene.
Remember those avocado toilets and those lovely
    matching sinks?
Funny how taste changes, Bill, it makes you really think.

I had a Perry Como cut, when I was just thirteen,
Thought it was the bees' knees; I was with it as a teen.
Italian suit, a knitted tie, Italian shoes as well,
An East End Mod, born really close to the famous old
    Bow Bells.

Lambretta or a Vespa was a serious choice to make,
Ska and R & B, Ted would always take the cake.
The Sixties, mate, were special; we thought we owned the
    world.
In lots of ways, I guess we did, every boy and girl.
Fashion, music, everything seemed to come from here.
Yeah, England was the place to be. D'ya want another
    beer?

Ships that pass in the night

You sail your memories across my seven seas,
Talking in shadows black, you reach to talk to me.
But how can I move to touch you,
When my body is far below you
And my spirit moves to get to you?
Oh, those ships that pass in the night,
Sail on, sweet mystery's flight.
Dreams, burned by the morning light,
So near, yet so far from home,
Too close to touch,
And all alone.

The burned-out bridges of the past are still in flame,
All battles won and lost, they end, to begin again.
Your banners fly so high, into the darkened sky.
My spirit moves on up to you,
Yeah, those ships that pass in the night,
Sail on, sweet mystery's flight.
Dreams, burned by the morning light,
So near, yet so far from home,
Too close to touch,
I'm on my own.

Music

Music is a wonderful thing, from the Classics
    to the songs we sing.
Moods enhanced, drama heightened, the
    darkest days can be lightened.
Majestic Wagner, Elgar, Mozart, so many
    more; where do I start
To thank you for your inspired gift? Your work
    the savage beast does lift.
Melodies soar into the sky, kissed by angels
    as they fly.
Tunes that bring you a memory, when you
    were young, footloose and free;
A song takes you back again, to a place or
    time with a distant friend.
Maybe you danced in a lover's arms; perhaps
    you fell beneath their charms
As the music played on that special day, a
    perfect time, I hear you say.
Carried off by magic wings, wings of music,
    notes that sing,
Of a time and place, back there and then,
    remembering, remembering.

Music plays in our strange world, Rock 'n'
Roll and boy meets girl.
Buddy Holly, Beatles tunes, underneath that
true blue moon.
A constant mistress, my life, my love, good
vibrations from above.
Thank you, music, you saved my soul, with
your Classics, Blues and Rock 'n' Roll.

Travelling tinker man

I never met you, my grandad, Tom – only
    faded photos of you in the drom.
I loved your wife and knew her well, sweet
    Nanny Kemp, Olive, Nell.

I wonder what you would think of me, of
    what I've done, of what I've been.
I feel your blood runs in my veins, blue eyes
    like mine, they look the same.

What did you see, what stories untold?
    A travelling man, big and bold.
How I wish, as a chav, I'd sat on your knee,
    as you told me of a land that was free.

The open road, a horse, a wagon. Another
    time when dreams could happen.
What would you think of this land, this time,
    when to live like you has become a
    crime?

Don't you worry, Tom, for in my sons, your
spirit lives, you travel on.
I thank you for what I am, Grandad Tom.
A travelling man from a distant drom.

Religion

Fires burning in the east, religion, God, philosophy,
From ages past they rear their heads, like ghosts arising
from the dead.
An eye for an eye, a tooth for a tooth. This can't be right,
where is the truth?
A holy mess of Man's making, where is this God,
When will he come to remedy what Man has done?
To right the wrongs, to bring the peace, a flight of angels
to release.
Put out this fire, stop this hate. Stop hatred now, before
it's too late.
Where is compassion, kindness, love? I thought that good
came from God above,
So why does the fire still burn in your soul, God-fearing
man, as death takes its toll?
Why no answer to your cries and needs?
As the women and children, like fugitives, flee,
As your brothers lie dying. For religion, you say.
It doesn't make sense, as you kneel and you pray.

Like moths to a flame

Look, that's him, look, over there,
I recognise him, with that long curly hair.
How I've waited for this; I'm gonna ask for a kiss.
You coming or not? Oh my God, he's so hot.
They said that he'd stay here, it's him, crystal clear.
I know that he'll like me, I'm his number one fan;
He'll remember me, won't he? He'll know who I am.
Are you coming, or not? Cos I'll go on my own.
Look! He's about to go in and he's there all alone.
Now is the moment, now is our chance,
What's wrong with you, girl, are you stuck in a trance?
Right now, that's it. Hello, over here.
Look, he's turning around, my God, he's so near.
My knees are a-shaking, what shall I say?
Oh no, it ain't him! Shall we go? No, let's stay.

Dad

You are my hero, you were my guide; I feel
    your love from the other side.
Happy days I spent with you, those
    memories keep flooding through.
Up on your shoulders, your strong hands,
    aboard those ships from foreign lands;
A font of wisdom, a don't do that, Golden
    Virginia, a trilby hat

The youngest child of thirteen others, a
    Scottish father and an English mother,
It must have been so tough for you,
    neglected, poor and without shoes,
But what a man you became, strong and
    decent, I bear your name.

You influenced me and taught me right,
    taught me how to stand and fight.
In the mirror now I look like you, looking
    back with your eyes of blue.
I'm proud of that, my hero dad, father, son,
    the love we had.

What days they were! Remember the time
    when all of us were doing fine.

They gave us a pre-fab, our very first house,
    in a street near the docks in old Custom
    House.
Mum made it a palace, she made it a home.
    We had no TV and no telephone,
But a garden to play in and a house full of
    love.
I know you're still there, looking down from
    above.

Firework night

Roman candles, jumping jacks, rocket to the
  stars,
Light touch-paper and retreat, as your rocket
  leaves for Mars.
I love Guy Fawkes, with his Catholic bomb;
  he gave us November the fifth.
Let the bonfire burn into the night, with him
  on top of it.
Sparkle, dazzle, oohs and aahs, as the
  Gunpowder Plot explodes.
When I was young, we'd never heard of this
  newfangled firework code.
Bangers would bang, sparklers spark,
  Catherine wheels would spin.
Rocket wars began as away we ran, me and
  my mate Jim.
We made a contraption a bit like a cannon,
  from a pipe and a piece of wood,
Load a ball bearing and some banger powder
  and it worked really good.
Roman candles held in your hand, the fiery
  balls would fly

Through the smoke-filled streets; it was really
neat, taking the girls by surprise.
What a time was had; I'm very glad health
and safety did not exist,
Cos we had fun, fun by the ton. It's good to
take a risk.

All along the watch tower

One two, one two, test.
Go round the toms, Dave,
That snare sounds the best.
Gerry, you're next; more, Reg, if you can,
Have a word with Gavin, he's your monitor man.

I remember you, Reg, though I called you Paul,
Standing out in front, in every hall,
Concerned and caring, while me and the boys
Blew you away with our musical toys.

Vibrations, reverb, EQs digital,
Tour manager, Reg, you did it all.
A mixer, a master, an opener of wine,
You made it happen – the show went on time.

No encore, just curtains and why, Reg, so soon?
Do the good die young, like you and Keith Moon?
I remember the goodbye, the degradable box,
All along the watch tower, Jimi rocks.
We could hardly believe it, the band and your friends.
Was this the last number, was this really the end?

I'm glad you came back with that message you sent,
Through that lady I met, in that mystical tent.
Yes, I've met him, I'm happy, that's what you said.
I've met Jimi; he's here, with some more of the dead.

It's gonna be all right

I believe in a light that shines bright,
I believe that a star will guide us through this night,
This very strange night.
I believe there's a path we'll find,
Memories we will leave behind, on this night,
This blackest night.
I hear you calling out to me,
I hear the wind whisper in the trees.
It's gonna be all right.

Here we stand with our world upside down,
Not a word, not a sigh, not a sound.
It's a very strange night.
All the plans that we thought we'd made,
All the dreams now seem to fade.
They're tumbling down, down to the ground.
I hear you calling out to me,
I hear the wind whisper in the trees,
It's gonna be all right.

Don't worry that the sun will rise;
Dry those tears, the tears you cry.

It's just a matter of time, things will be fine.

We have love, it will see us through.

Look, you're smiling, look at you.

The sun will rise, so dry your eyes.

I hear you calling out to me,

I hear the wind whisper in the trees.

It's gonna be all right.

Maybe it's because I'm a Londoner

I remember that foggy morning, the East
    End, cobbled street,
Long shorts, knitted jumper and sandals on
    my feet.
This was it, the lorry trip, off to another
    world,
Where birds can sing, where cows are milked
    by pretty country girls.

Now climb on the lorry, folks; get on, there's
    loads of room.
We will be through Blackwall Tunnel and get
    to Kent by noon.
On through the famous tunnel in a cloud of
    blue exhaust,
To trees and fields and fresher air. Look,
    Mum! There's a horse.

Country lanes, they look like cows. I saw a
    haystack, Mum.
Well, make a wish, it might come true. Sit
    down, be careful, son.

We trundle on, up over hills and over greener
dales.
A band of Cockneys singing songs, the wind
now in our sails.

Through the garden, garden of England, from
old London town.
A lorryload of hop pickers, a bushel for a
pound.
Down the dirt track, to the farm, on to the
sheds we go,
To find our bunks in our new home, pronto,
toe to toe.

Fill the mattress full of hay, the farmhand
leads the way;
Find our bunks, it's home from home for our
country stay.
Grown ups talk of this and that, kids still full
of life;
Bedtime now, get washed and changed,
everything's all right.

Time now, boy, to hit the hay, tomorrow's a
    big day.
There's work to do, hops to pick and you
    need to earn your pay.
Communal wash, pyjamas on, I climb into
    my bed.
Now off to sleep, Mum says to me. Come on
    now, sleepyhead.
Drifting off, I can hear the sound of the
    campfire's crackling glow,
Conversations, a song or two, from voices
    I don't know.

At the crack of dawn a cockerel crows, it's as
    if he seems to know
It's time to rise, open up your eyes and off to
    work you go.
Mum's impressed, I'm washed and dressed,
    ready, willing and able.
We leave the hut, Mum, Nanny and me and
    pass the horses' stable.
My Nan's been picking hops in Kent,
    probably all her life;

She loves it here, she knows the ropes, the
    tinker's little wife.

The pole man says a warm hello to Nan and
    Mum and me.
I bet the boy won't pick too much, he'll be
    off climbing a tree.
The tall hop vines, the happy times, the bins
    soon full of hops,
My Nan and Mum, having fun, as the picking
    never stops.

I pick a few, like you do, but pretty soon I see
A boy I know from Custom House, half way
    up a tree.
I disappear from the smell of beer into the
    autumn air.
It was brilliant and different my hopping
    holiday. Yeah!

The pavilion

We sat in the pavilion, well, really a shed.
It should brighten up later, somebody said.
The rain, like a cloudburst, rattled the roof.
Ginger then said, I've got a bad tooth,
If we do go out to play, I don't want to bowl.
I'll bat if you like, I'll honour my role.

It's lightening up, the sun's breaking through,
Let's toss up and play, if it's all right with
        you.
The butcher, the builder, the geography
        teacher prepared to enter the fray.
I'll open this end, the end with wind, said fast
        bowler Ray.

All dressed in white, let's keep it tight, no
        singles and stay on your toes.
Ball number one, a crack of the bat, leather
        against willow.
Off to mid-on, almost a catch, but a beautiful
        return throw.

This game is tradition, this game is the
    Empire, played in sister lands.
It is more than a game, a sport that is
    sporting. That ball just went to hand!

Cerebral, physical, as the scoreboard
    changes to a wicket or a four,
Where victors and losers will meet for a beer
    and banter just like before.
Talk about tactics and their teammates'
    antics. I'll see ya, I can't really stay.
Can you play next week? I'll let you know,
    is it home, or is it away?

All the pennies in the world

All the pennies in the world and a jugful, that's what you
    mean to me;
Those sparkling eyes, those gypsy eyes, warm and bright
    and free.
A wonderful one, the sacrifice, the tragic stolen years;
You gave and gave in every way, holding back your tears.
Every thought and wish you dreamed were meant for me
    alone,
Forgive the way it had to end, for I couldn't face the truth.
I should have been there, there with you, under the same
    roof.

Well, all is fine, the kids are good, growing every day.
I know you keep an eye on them, in your special way.
You dancing girl, you grandmother, I miss you every day.
So many things bring memories, but all I want to say
Is, you are great, I miss you, mate and I hope you are OK.
Fly the moon, autumn leaves drift by your window now;
A can can kick, a clever trick; dear Dolly, take a bow.

Shining stars

Josef, Daisy, George, David, Sophie and Finlay,
Like shining stars fell into my life.
One by one they fell from heaven and lit every dark
    moment.
Some giggled, some smiled, some cried for a while,
Some ran like the wind, mile upon mile.

Treasures of the future, heartaches to come,
I would love to be there when their races are run.
What adventures, what dreams, what lives to be had,
I hope some remember their silly Grandad.

The one with a story, the one with a tale
Of dragons and knights, over hill, over dale.
Of ice creams and chocolates, when Mummy said no.
When the world said stop, I was the one that said go.

There on the touchline, still there when I'm gone,
Watching from somewhere just how they get on.
Guiding and hoping their dreams will come true,
My daughter and sons will help them pull through.
So blessed with their laughter and to comfort their tears,
Just make sure they are special, in the long coming years.

Silver bird

I get on a plane now and again, but never
     understand why
A big silver bird of metal and stuff can ever
     actually fly.
There are bags in the hold, folk in the cabin,
     tons of fuel inside,
So how does it do it, fly like a bird, up into
     the sky?

Down the runway it goes, carrying its load,
     with a roar and a muted scream;
Up and away through the grey sky we fly,
     in Man's flying machine,
To horizons new, where the sky is so blue and
     seat belts duly fastened.
With the land far below, upwards we go,
     bemused and a little bit frightened.
But dinner is served, as the plane takes a
     swerve, somewhere over Ireland.

There are films on board too, to help us get
     through that horrible, endless flight.

Merrily we go, packed head to toe, on and
into the night.
The glamour is past, like cows in a shed and
sardines packed real tight.
When I get off this thing, I'm really hoping
this flight will be my last.
We start our descent, when orders are sent,
as clouds go rushing past.

We finally land, near the sea and the sand,
and depart the giant bird.
Broken and bent, red-eyed and spent, to
security I'm referred.
So I join the big queue, with the cattle that
flew, reasonably undeterred.
There was glamour once, I bet there was, a
civilised, stately trip.
If I don't get out of this airport real soon,
I think I'm gonna flip.

Remembrance

He stood at the Cenotaph, old but not bent,
Remembering, just remembering.
His medals shone brightly, his beret pristine,
Watching the ceremony, surveying the scene.
Old soldiers en masse, warriors all,
Standing like oak trees, strong now and tall.
A wreath full of poppies, a tribute to men;
In homage to them, he remembers again,
The shell-shocked, the lost, the forgotten lost souls.
He holds back the tears, the eleventh hour tolls.
Those wars to end war, for freedom, for all;
We must never forget, those that would fall.
Those men and those women, he remembers the time
When the washing was hung on the Siegfried Line,
When pals watched your back, when Lucifers lit,
When Tommy screamed, when Tommy was hit.
He remembers and wonders, why them and not me?
I made it back, to dear old Blighty.
We danced in the streets that were broken and torn;
We hugged and we kissed, as a new age was born.
He stands and remembers, as tributes are laid
And hopes in his heart that their memory won't fade.

Beano day

Oi Mum, what's today? Is today Beano day?
Get ready for school, that's all Mum would say.
But it's Thursday, I said, it is Beano day.
That's tomorrow, you stinker; today is Wednesday.
Oh blimey, I said, with a big grumpy frown,
I thought it was Thursday, wot a let down.
Here's your football shirt, son, now go comb your hair.
Where's me football boots, Mum?
Open your eyes! Over there.
Are you watching the match? Cos Dad is at work;
I reckon we'll win. Where d'ya put my shirt?
I don't think I can, son; I've got too much to do.
Get ready now, please, cos I'm waiting for you.
I think I was supposed to take back that book,
The one that I borrowed, the one Jimmy took.
Did you read it yet? No, not really, Mum,
It looked a bit boring. Please hurry up, son.
Now here is your lunch and I've put in a drink.
I can buy me a jubbly, I've got money, I think;
They sell them frozen, they're really nice.
You should try one, Mum, it's like orangey ice.
I love you, Mum. I love you, son.

Now give us a kiss and off you run.
Be good and careful. I will. Don't forget –
The key to get in is under the step.

The boxer

Rolling with the punches, ducking and diving,
Gladiators, versed in the art of boxing;
With fury, with skill, with honour at stake,
Respecting the fighter, but with a point now to make.
The pre-fight and weigh-in, fight training was tough,
Both boxers hoping that they did enough.
The sweat and the blood, the roar of the ringside,
There's nowhere to run now and nowhere to hide;
The smell of the leather, the cut men are poised,
There in the corner to repair the brave boys.
The hall full of fans, baying for a knock out,
Jab, jab and move, the old fighter shouts,
Clearing his head and using the ropes,
For pride and the family, for a title hope.
A left to the body, a right to the jaw,
The worthy contender folds to the floor,
Hitting the canvas. The ref starts to count;
His head in a spin, his legs given out;
Eight, nine and ten and now it's done.
The winner on shoulders, well done, son.
The fighters embrace, with respect for each other,
Bloodied and bruised; respect for you, brother.

Celebrity

Don't call me a celebrity,
I don't need an A list, B or C,
I don't do jungles or cooking programmes,
I'm only a man, doing what I can.
I just write songs and sing a bit,
Sometimes an actor, when I'm legit.

Music, theatre, film and stuff,
What I do ain't all that tough.
Lucky for me, some people care;
I'd like to thank you all out there.

Please don't call me a celebrity,
I'm not a Big Brother entity.
Fame for fame, what's in a name?
Translucent emptiness.
Entourage and chauffeured cars,
One big pretentious mess.

I've always tried to do my best,
In case you showed any interest.
It's thanks to you that I've stayed true,

Cos you gave me the freedom to create.
My destiny, my journey too,
My personal fate was sealed by you.
But something, someone is looking down,
To help and guide through Tinseltown.

Rock on

Hey did ya Rock 'n' Roll, rock on, ooh my soul,
Hey did ya boogie too, did ya?

Hey shout summertime blues,
Jump up and down in your blue suede shoes,
Hey did you Rock 'n' Roll, rock on.

And where do we go from here,
Which is the way that's clear?

Still looking for that blue jean baby queen,
Prettiest girl I've ever seen,
See her shake on the movie screen, Jimmy Dean.

Hey look, the leader of the pack,
Tattooed smile, leather on your back,
Rebel, rebel, blackboard jungle,
Rock on.

Over the rainbow

Over the rainbow, run through the rain, good to get back
    to home once again.
We looked for a long day, but no pot of gold; we were
    brave to set forth, braver than bold.
I did have reservations, I think you had too, but at least
    we saw grey sky turn into blue.
Just think if we'd found it, a pot full of gold, a life-
    changing sum, a life off the dole.
But money can't buy happy, money can't buy love; as it is,
    we are blessed by something above.
Family and friends, good health on the whole, a bun in
    the oven and a contented soul.
Those older and wiser, when I was a boy, said material
    wealth does not bring us joy.
I thought they were wrong, questioned their stance; I'd
    have money to burn if I had the chance.
But to see the sun rise, to hear the birds sing is more
    precious to us than money and things.
Still I think of that rainbow when the going gets tough,
But the family and friends are more than enough.

The boy

The boy's got charisma, the boy's got real charm;
We could offer a contract, it would do no harm.
I've just got this feeling, he's gonna go far;
I think given time he could be a star.

He can act, he can sing; we could teach him to dance,
Buy him some clothes, his image enhance;
Get him writing some songs, some hits would be good.
With commercial bits in them, I think that we could
Record a hit single, it wouldn't take long;
All that we need is a bloody good song.

The boy's really got it, no worries about that.
If he don't become big, I'll eat my mum's hat.
He's a star in the making, a giving cash cow;
He just needs some guidance, a bit of know how.
So son, here's your deal; just sign and you'll see,
Your life will be changed if you stick with me.

Flash cars, houses, ladies galore,
Just sign this contract to open the door.
Our office, our staff are all fans of yours;

My massive percentage – I could ask for more –
But I believe you can make it, make it in time.
Take my gold pen and sign on the line.
No thanks.

Upton Park

Gotta go now, Dad, gotta go; line up, gotta
    line up for the game.
I think we'll win, with Keeble and Dick, but
    I think it's going to rain.
Can I have two bob for the bus and a hot
    dog? I'll pay you back real soon.
The Hammers are playing Newcastle, Dad,
    I think they're called the Toon.
You should see it there, Upton Park,
    thousands in claret and blue,
And the blokes let kids in down the front,
    dockers just like you.
They sing and cheer with their fags and beer,
    blowing bubbles to a man;
When a goal goes in you should hear the din,
    East London, our West Ham.
There's magic in the stadium, there's magic
    in the air,
Is it true that once upon a time, Anne Boleyn
    lived there?
I bet she'd be a West Ham fan, if she was
    here today;

But her castle's gone, she must have moved,
     so the boys could get to play.
I saw some players in the cafe, when I was in
     Green Street,
John Bond, Ken Brown and Noel Cantwell,
     sitting in their seats.
They signed my book and said hello; it was
     great, Dad, really good.
I've gotta go, I can't be late; we'll win today,
     we should.

The sea

Standing out at the water's edge, the waves
    kissing the shore,
Looking out to sea, you see, for a ship or
    maybe more.
A great white whale, a shoal of fish like
    diamonds in the sun;
Neptune's crown, a pirate ship, armed with
    swords and guns.

A water world, strange, unknown, Atlantis
    fathoms deep;
Davy Jones' locker, locked with secrets
    there to keep.
To think that this same rolling sea will reach
    America,
My message in a bottle, would it get that far?

The driftwood on this empty beach could
    come from anywhere,
Hong Kong or Greece, Africa, among the
    fruits de mare.

The stories that this sea could tell, of
    battles won and lost,
Of those that perished in its wake, those
    lost at such a cost;
Of battleships, of sailors' lives, sunk
    without a trace,
Explorers just like Captain Cook, floating
    round the place.

The lighthouse, with its guiding light,
    beckons us to shore,
Through sea mist, storm and tempest rage,
    to reach the land once more.
What secrets does this sea withhold, what
    bounty in its keep?
A watery world of mystery, below the ocean
    deep;
Treasure, shipwrecks, mariners lost, as
    widows gently weep.

Cowboy

This is weird, this is strange, riding across the vast
    prairie range,
Under a big hat, on top of a horse, hanging on for
    dear life;
I'm a cowboy, of course.
Rootin' and tootin', just like that John Wayne,
Whose real name was Marion; there's a lot in a name.

My revolver is cocked and I'm ready to shoot;
When I finds me a stagecoach, I'm taking the loot.
I'm mean and I'm bad and dangerous to know,
A bit like Lord Byron from years long ago.

I'm gonna fill ya with lead, gonna shoot it all out;
Gonna swing that lasso, gonna holla and shout;
Gonna build a camp fire and cook me some chow,
Gonna chew some tobaccy, gonna round up a cow.

I like baked beans for breakfast, some black coffee too.
My horse is a palomino, but I call him Blue.
A pioneer in this country, this brand new frontier,
Heading west with the rest, riding out without fear.

OK, it's a movie, just a few frames,
The Wild West is broken, broken and tamed,
But there's a wolf on the prowl still,
And a horse with no name.
Cut, very good, but let's try that again.

Are you still my true love?

Girl, you say your love is strong,
Stronger than an oak tree,
But I feel there's something wrong,
Your eyes no longer look to me.
The pale moon high in the autumn sky,
Don't seem to give an answer.
Is your love still strong?
Is there something wrong?
Are you still my true love?

When we walked in the summer sun,
You smiled your smile so sweetly.
Hand on hand, I was the one,
You'd always run to meet me.
With your dancing eyes, was your truth a lie?
How could you betray me?
See the pale moon high in the summer sky;
Are you still my true love?

When winter brings its icy winds,
Love, will you be leaving?
When the robins fly in the cold grey sky,

What will I be seeing?
A love still strong, or a love gone wrong?
Only you can answer.
See the pale moon high in the winter sky,
Are you still my true love? Are you still the one?
See the pale moon high in the winter sky,
Are you still my true love?

My three sons

My three sons, handsome boys, take after their mums;
My three sons,
Sharp and quick, strong and bright, up to tricks,
From noon to night.
If I said I was proud, that's an understatement;
If I told them I loved them, there'd be a hint of
     embarrassment.
But I do, you see, I do very much,
From cradle to football pitch, from boy to man.
Just a very proud father, that's what I am.

Like my father before me, they carry my name;
With their own sons now, do they feel the same?
What a blessing they've been, my three sons,
For me, their dad and their beautiful mums.

We have had our moments, with this spirited three;
When it comes down to it, they're a lot like me.
Rascals sometimes, angels too; it seems that all monkeys
Are not in the zoo.
Would I change a thing about Bill, Kit and Dan?
Certainly not, cos they made me a man.

Just watching them grow into the young men they are,
Smiling inside as they follow their star,
Finding themselves and winning the game;
My three sons, they carry my name.

Love after love

Love will rise like a phoenix from emptiness,
Love will bring light, where there were shadows.
Healing hurts with its truth; Love, reaching out with a
    strength not felt when alone.
A spark that will light and comfort and lift the lonely soul,
Love remains pure,
Love remains true,
And once more, love has come to you.

Oh suburbia!

Just before the day is dawning,
He comes back, tired and yawning;
She gets up to make the coffee,
He kicks the dog and then says sorry.

Strange the day, the shadows whisper,
The milkman whistles at your sister.
Oh suburbia! How I love ya.
Sunday morning and I'm washing my Cortina,
Think I'll turn the radio on
And listen to my favourite song;
All the hits and groovy DJs,
Making me happy, they're making my day.

Meet the boys in a pub by the river;
Super Sunday, will the team deliver?
The barmaid here is really tasty,
I will make a move, but don't wanna be hasty.
We're one goal down and the team is looking shaky.
Oh suburbia! How I love ya;
Sunday morning and I'm washing my Cortina.

Opening night

Well this is it, the opening night, a mix of
    excitement and nervous fright;
The dress rehearsal was a mess, fingers
    crossed, hope for the best.
An extra week would have been good,
    under-rehearsed, I think we could
Have worked that scene to make it tight,
    but here we go on the opening night.
Family, friends, are in tonight; let's tell our
    story and reach the heights,
Previews were very strong, they seem to like
    the closing song.
Reviews I never read; a critic's choice is just
    one voice.
And after all, what do they know, about the
    qualities of a show?
Five minutes please, beginners now, time to
    take that opening bow;
Curtain up, lights on stage, the stage
    manager turns the page.
So here we go, on with the show, let's break
    a leg, yes this is it;

One big breath, yes this is it; the MD watches
    from the pit.
Act One is done, it went so well, Act Two
    begins, the bar bells
Summon all into the stalls, to watch again
    the rise and fall,
To laugh and cry, to enter in a wonderland;
    let us begin.
A pin could drop, there is no sound, the
    curtain now is coming down.
We did our best, they're on their feet; they
    roar and clap, ovation sweet.
We bow to say that we thank you, for your
    warmth tonight,
It helped us through.

Painted clown

Behind that mask, painted clown, lies
      tragedy, scars of the past,
Hidden now, away from light, behind that
      mask painted white.
They poke you with their knives and sticks,
      crucify you just for kicks,
Buffoon, jester, make me laugh; help me
      kill the fatted calf.
Son of God you say I am; dance for me,
      you painted clown.
Show me tricks, now part the waves; smile
      for me, you jester knave.
I see tears rolling down, did someone steal
      your thorny crown?
King of fools, king of clowns, stop your
      tears from tumbling down.
Your kingdom came, painted clown,
      wisdom spoken, wise words said,
Voices whispered in your head; the king is
      dead, long live the king,
Walk upon the water, then

Let us sing, dance and rejoice; let us speak
with just one voice.
Clown you are, make me smile, amuse me
now, show me how;
Play for me, tumble, fall; give to me your
kingdoms all.
Somersault through purple haze, lead me
to your altar blaze.
Burn your churches to the ground, it's only
bricks, the choir's sound.
Noble clown, look now you're down, down,
down in Devil's Drive;
Praise to him, begin to sing; the clown is
still alive.

On and on

You're like a song,
A song that comes and goes and then is gone,
A melody that seems to linger on;
You're on and on, you're my song.

A magic spell,
A shooting star that sounds like a silver bell,
Something out of heaven must have fell,
You're on and on, you're my song.

A clown can cry, the tears will fill our eyes,
The memories that you've seen, are made of velveteen.
Your yesterdays have gone, but yesterdays live on;
You're on and on.

Oh let it ring, the magical magician gets to sing;
Let me be your blue-eyed harlequin,
Because you're on and on.
You're my song.

Flamingo

The pavement shook from the beat below,
     as I lined up for the Flamingo.
An all-night show of rhythm and blues,
     purple hearts, kick off your shoes.
I didn't know what to expect, as I went
     downstairs, circumspect.
The place was packed, the joint did jump,
     as the Blue Flames' music began to
     pump.
The walls were wet, wet with sweat; the
     dance floor jammed, rammed and yet,
I knew right then this felt like home,
     as I stood there, watching on my own.
Like that famous star over Bethlehem,
     shining in the night,
This is the way, it seemed to say;
     Zoot Money's got it right.
Wide-eyed, legless at six a.m., I climbed
     those famous stairs,
From Wardour Street to Canning Town,
     I walked the cool dawn air,

My mind made up, my future planned,
    shell-shocked with happiness,
As the East End woke; the morning folk
    just wouldn't understand,
I've got a plan, I've seen the light;
    I'm gonna join a band.

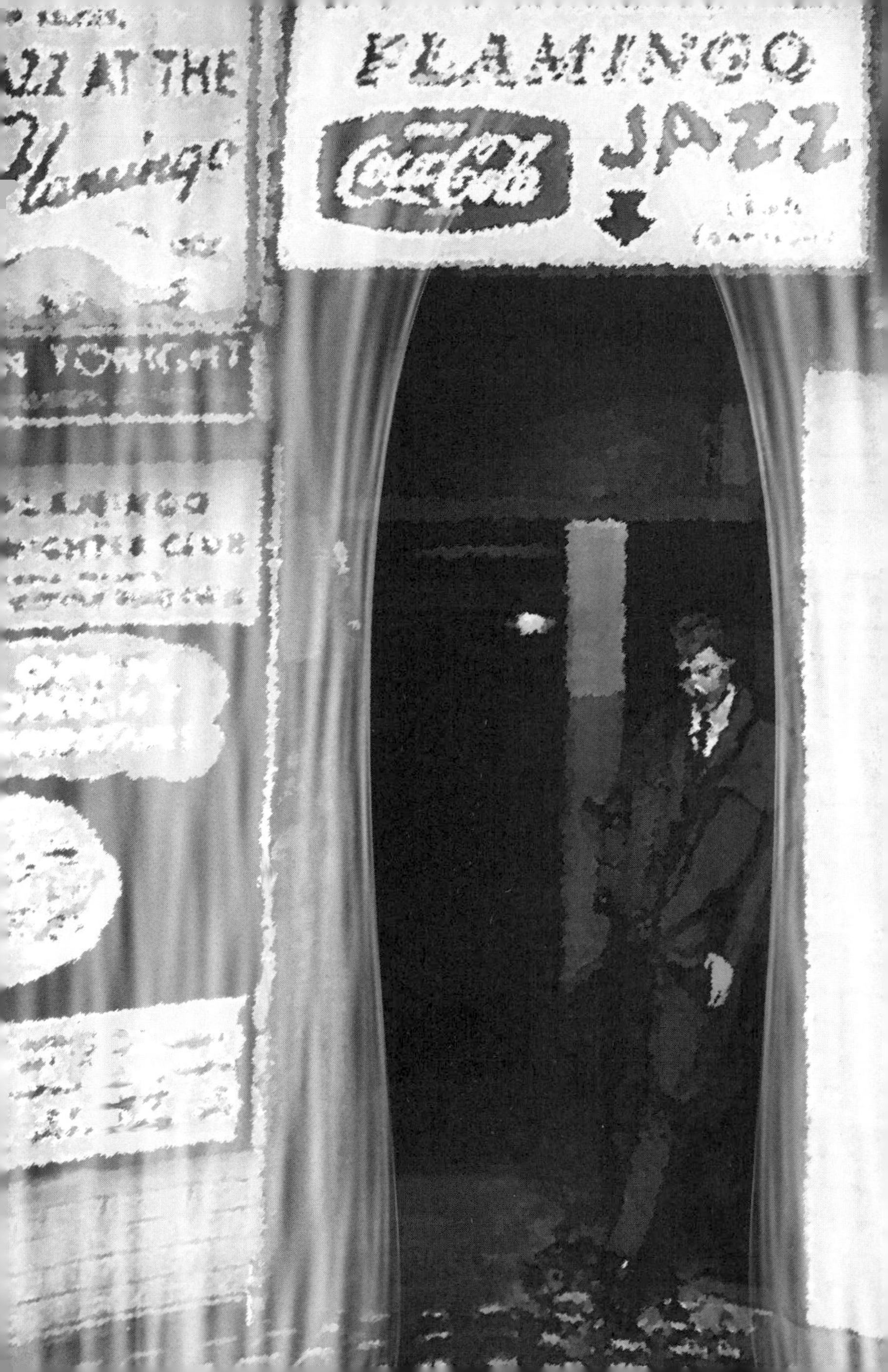

FLAMINGO
Coca-Cola
JAZZ
AT THE

Shooting star

Can you see that shooting star, there in the
    night sky, proud and high?
Make a wish, it may come true, it's falling from
    the sky for you.
Take care though, friend, in what you wish,
    sometimes a wish,
Like a distant kiss, is cold, and never ever
    missed.

But make that wish for all mankind, a selfless
    gesture that will shine.
Whisper now, or shout it loud, make that wish
    to make us proud;
Freedom from hunger, war and strife, make a
    wish to change their life.
Don't waste that wish, it may come true, as did
    that fallen star for you.

Summer rain, wash away their pain and freshen
    up the mourning air.
Your wish for people will bring rewards,
    sometime, somehow, somewhere.

It is your wish, it belongs to you, use wisely,
    for good, not greed.
Perhaps that wish will bring some good,
    some hungry mouths to feed.
Did you see that falling star, from the hilltop
    where we are?
Yes, I think from way up here, that wish seems
    crystal clear.

Into the woods

Into the woods, a magical place,
Where the green man lives, without a face,
Where twilight is king, where the trees softly speak
Of creatures that crawl and creatures that seek.

The sun through the trees, the life-giving sun,
Hidden from sight, the fox on the run,
The badgers that mount, the pixie that dances,
The butterfly full of life's fleeting chances.

The frog by the stream, in wait for a princess,
The quick-running hare, shrouded in shyness,
The owl in his wisdom refuses to sing,
A squawk of contempt as the magpie takes wing.

The bounce of the bunny, the branches that sway
In the trees that were planted in olden days,
The tree trunks with faces older than time
Looked down on the limb the schoolboy did climb.

But the night shift has started,
In the wood's moon shadows,

The residents restless, the forest's stream flows.
The mole in the bank rubs sleepy eyes,
The blackbird sings in the treetop up high.
A little bit scary, a little bit strange,
The atmosphere suddenly begins to change.
A rustle of leaves, a slither of snake,
The creatures of night begin to awake.

Bankers

Bankers are wankers, that conveniently rhymes,
Helping us through bleak fiscal times,
Stocking those shares, hedging their bets,
Stashing the dosh, grabbing all they can get.

Dog eat dog, profit and loss, materialism, capitalism,
Corporate bandits, Footsie toe rags,
Stashing your dosh in their money bags.
Compassion for money, sentiment for greed,
We stand at your gate, our children to feed.
Speculate, investigate, bonus me up,
Give me it all, fill up my cup.
It's all about money, buy now and sell.
Vultures get ready for the opening bell.

Let's make a killing, your investment is safe.
You don't have to worry, cos we fix the rate.
Recession, don't worry, my bonus is secure,
Just think what you'll make when your pension matures.

Ethics, don't think so, not really my thing,
I want to make millions before the fat lady sings.
It's just like Las Vegas, a gambling den,
But we wear a nice suit and a tie now and then,
To look like professionals, sensible men.
Trust me, don't worry, here – use my pen.

Of course rates may vary, fees may change too,
Don't worry, we'll monitor the funds you withdrew.
We must charge you charges, we need to get fat;
I want a Ferrari and my wife wants a hat.

Ricky and Carol

Rock 'n' Roll is here to stay, Blue Suede Shoes,
That'll Be The Day,
On Route 66, We Got Our Kicks,
With stolen beats from R & B,
Jitter bug jump for you and me,
Pink-frocked girls with beehive hair,
Boys' beetle crushed, would stand and stare.

Do you like Gene Vincent, do you like Dion?
Yeah, I think The Wanderer is a real neat song.
Do you wanna dance, can you do the jive?
Does your heart beat fast, do you feel alive?

I love that Elvis, he's the one for me.
Nah, I think he died when he joined the army.
Shangri La, the leader, Leader of the Pack,
Will Jimmy never ever be coming back?

Bonneville, Norton, BSA Gold Star,
Ford Zodiac, cushti two-toned dream car;
Knuckleduster, flick knife and tattooed smile,
As Ricky and Carol walk down the church aisle.

Working men's club

It was Saturday night in the working men's club;
The snooker was snookered as the band began to play,
A song from Al Jolson, a tune from the past,
A popular choice, not slow or too fast,
As memories floated, like fluffy white clouds,
In the smoke-filled room of memories past.

Brown ale and some crisps, give us a song;
Come on now, you lot, all sing along.
The foxes would trot, the gay Gordons dance,
In front of the stage, the band in a trance,
Like robots, well worn by the waltzes of time;
In an hour or so you'll see, all will be fine.

It's bingo, eyes down and get ready,
Says our rosy-cheeked master of the bingo ceremony.
The band take a break for a beer and a ciggie,
And chat up the gals in hope of jiggy jiggy.
Full house over here, says a voice in the dark,
As the drummer and lady disappear to the park.

These are my people, grandads and nans,
Fathers and mums, woman and man.
It's our Saturday shindig, a knees up for all,
Look at him, George, he's got really tall
How old are you now, son? You're growing up fast.
Must be school dinners, that voice from the past.

They ruffle your hair, they give you a wink,
Hold up their glass, buy you a drink.
The band has come back, the muzak plays on,
Any requests for tonight's final song?
Embarrassed, awkward, as the last waltz plays,
Dragged to the dance floor by Mum's loving gaze.

Goodbye first love

Did you fall, was there pain, has your heart
    been broken again?
It seemed so right at the time, your
    soulmate, friend, so sweet and kind.
The hurt will pass, though, it's for the best.
    Looking back, you could have guessed
You'd be let down; it's no surprise, if you
    looked into those lying eyes.
What did you see, was your love blind,
    didn't you realise you'd be left behind?
But you are young, today will pass and
    you will find love, a love to last.
I know that first love is very strong,
    but someone else will come along.
Out of the blue, you'll find the one;
    when you least expect it, love will come.
Today's heartache will be forgotten;
    I understand that you feel rotten,
But look at you, so much to give.
    Forget it now, move on and live.

Levi

A wag of the tail, a wiggle of the bum,
A look in those brown eyes, come on, let's have fun.
A big welcome home, a dog with a bone,
Levi the dog, you run and you roam.

Full of adventure, a growl and a bark,
A prankster, hellbent on having a lark;
A squirrel to chase and football to play,
Look out for the traffic. Good boy – now stay.

A love that seems selfless, a leader of the pack,
But why, when I call you, don't you come back?
A gift from a traveller, Charlie my friend,
A chase round the corner, a chase round the bend.

Poop scooper at dusk, a hunter at dawn,
Asleep in my bed, a big doggy yawn.
There's your mates in the park, Elvis and Jack,
Tuppence and Hodge, they're all in your pack.

I'm so glad I met you, my little friend,
Through the streets of old London, we march off again.
This tree looks interesting, this tree needs a pee,
And I'm the one to do it; it's good to be me.

Autumn

Falling leaves of red and gold float like
    memories, like feathers.
The last pale sun of summer glows,
    distancing itself from us below.
Autumn mist, harvest in, we wait for
    the icy winter to begin.
But here today, in all their glory, the falling
    leaves will tell their story,
Of summer past, of seaside trips, of Ninety
    Nines and Kiss Me Quicks,
Holiday romance, B & B, barbecue, picnics,
    clotted cream tea.
But there is something about this season,
    the autumn, the fall,
That touches me deeper and when I recall
The smell and the colour of this mystical
    season,
There's a place in my heart I feel I should
    mention.
This is my time now, yes this is my life,
    the autumn of my years;
Spring was special, summer too, but now
Toward winter, I look to you.

Artisans

Don't know about you, but whenever I view
    a new build, shiny and new,
They don't measure up; they don't look as
    good, well maybe just a few,
But most of the time the look and design
    seems to me inferior,
Characterless, anonymous, with a
    minimalist interior.
Where did they go, the artisans that built
    our heritage buildings,
With care and pride our country wide,
    their noble, grand beginnings?

I know a build not far from here; it's orange
    and lime green.
The architect won an award; it's the ugliest
    thing I've ever seen.
I remember, as a little boy, watching our
    streets changing
Into high rise, impersonal blocks. They told
    us they were amazing.

Now, as I walk in London town, with
    buildings like New York,
It's good to see, occasionally, architecture
    with some thought.
Nash and Wren, come back again, teach
    them style and taste.
These modern things have lost something,
    character and grace.

City boy

When you're young it's only natural,
You would want to accumulate capital,
Wealth and stuff, cars and bling
Seem to be the important thing.
Tomorrow, today is what you need,
No time to waste, you follow, I'll lead.
The latest gadget, the next best thing,
A really sharp suit, a platinum ring.
Forget about family, forget about health,
What's more important than rolling in wealth?

I want a Bentley, a penthouse too,
Some sparkling investments should make that come true.
Dog eating dog, digging for gold,
It's all about money, before I get old.

But when that day comes, as years drift on by,
Will wealth buy you health? I think that's a lie.
The family you left in second place,
Where are they now that you've won your race?
Forget the rat race, the materialism,
There's more to life than capitalism.

Cherish the family, the friends that you know,
The natural things, the sunset's red glow,
The moon, the stars, the life-giving rain.
Jump off that treadmill and just think again.

Fairies in the garden

There are fairies in the garden, Dad,
    there are, it's really true;
I saw them dancing, singing, dressed in
    pink and blue.
I wouldn't have believed it, but I saw it
    with my eyes;
I heard their lovely singing, I heard their
    quiet sighs.
They danced in a ring, together by the
    pond,
I reckon someone special must have waved
    a magic wand.
Do you think that they had seen me,
    hiding behind a tree?
I wonder if they know my name; d'ya think
    they know it's me?
I am really pleased they live here; Daddy,
    don't you think
We're lucky just to have them, shall I take
    them out a drink?

What do fairies eat, Dad? Flowers, berries
        and things?
I can't believe I saw them there, dancing
        in a ring.

Troubadours

You troubadours, you played along, with
      every beat to every song.
In studios, on stages too, there was I and
      there was you.
I brought the spark, you lit the fire, the riff,
      the chord, take a flyer.
A wall of sound, a rock of ages, psycho
      sound, the machine that rages.

Colour the ghost, touch it if you can, there in
      the shadows and so it began.
Those nights together, the smoke, the lights,
      so many concerts, so many late nights,
Arena, theatre and dressing rooms, waiting
      to play those popular tunes.

Brothers in music, brothers in kind, me up
      front and you behind.
Dedicated and motivated, together we
      have fun;
Another song, play along, could be a
      Number One.

In after four, let's try the bridge; there's still
        some beers left in the fridge.
I like this key, it works for me. Let's go again,
        let's try it and see.
Yeah, that feels good, yeah that feels right,
        let's do it in the show tonight.
Thank you one, thank you all, you
        troubadours, it's been real cool.

Like a rolling stone

My grandad was a traveller man, a tinker
    I'm told, Irish and bold.
I think his blood runs through my veins,
    as here I am, on the road again.
A tour, a suitcase, another city; I reckon
    old Tom would be quite proud of me.
I've travelled each and every road of our
    British isle, mile upon mile.
I've seen north, south, east and west and
    I reckon Britain is still the best.
From Leeds to Brighton, Cardiff to Poole,
    now I've got sat nav, I'm nobody's fool.
Way up to Scotland and down to Cornwall,
    Birmingham, Stoke, yes, I've seen them all.
Europe is nice, the USA too, Africa, India,
    I've travelled them through.
Something different, something to see; in
    Uganda they've got upside down trees.
I love to travel, like to move on; Like a Rolling
    Stone, that's one of my songs.
Down Under is great, the sun always shines,
    but it's a long way to go, takes a long time.

South America I think is a wonderful place,
     there is something about that Latin race,
Cuba Libre, Costa Rica, Bossa Nova,
     Che Guevara,
Mile upon mile, smile upon smile; traveller,
     rest. Rest for a while.

La la land

The Indian Ocean sighs under this different moon;
Should I reflect upon this moment, here, lost and
    marooned?
A strange foreign sound then pierces the night,
As a bird full of freedom, takes wing, now in flight.
To the stars she will fly, to the star-covered sky,
Under the gaze of the moon, fly freedom, fly.

Distance can bring objectivity;
Tonight on this shore, by the whispering sea,
My mistakes and my worries gently ebb like the tide,
Stowed in a treasure chest, thrown over the side.
Am I Robinson Crusoe? I've been here before.
Or the famed Mr Christian, on a lone distant shore?

I wait for a galleon, or a seahorse to ride,
A mermaid to kiss, to caress and confide.
Shall I tell of adventures, of pieces of gold,
Say I'm king of the pirates, handsome and bold?
Together we dive, beneath the blue waves,
Searching for pearls in a pink coral grave.

We swim with the dolphins, we ride a great whale,
While I search the horizon for a ship's friendly sail.
But what if we find it and rescued I'd be,
Chained for all time to reality?
At this moment I'm happy, at this time content
To swim with the flow, wherever I'm sent.

My mermaid will take me to the sea from the shore,
As ten fathoms deep, beneath the sea's roar,
There lies an answer, which waits to be found,
Is this world really flat, or really quite round?

Time machine

Wouldn't you love a time machine, that
　　　transported you to another scene?
Back in time to days gone by, back to Rome
　　　away you'd fly.
A week in Athens, Ancient Greece,
　　　searching for that Golden Fleece.
In London streets, in times of yore, to places
　　　never seen before.
In France to join the revolution, talk with
　　　Darwin, Evolution.
See dinosaurs, mammoths too, Dickens'
　　　days and World War Two.
Meet your grandad and grand mum, fly
　　　about and just have fun.
See how life was really lived, in those years,
　　　the ones you missed.
See the Ancient Pyramids built, the Tower
　　　of Pisa before the tilt,
Endless wonder, endless flight, back in time
　　　to see the sights.
Lancelot, Queen Guinevere, meet King
　　　Arthur for a beer.

Join the Gold Rush way out west, play
    football with Georgie Best,
Imagination is transportation, taking you
    to another location;
Use it well and do be wise, imagination
    opens eyes.
Meet me then in Babylon, imagination can't
    be wrong.

R.S.V.P.

I don't like parties, functions and dos,
There is a bit too much posturing, too much who's who.
I don't really drink and I'd rather not dance,
I'd give it a miss if I get the chance.
When they lay the red carpet, RSVP,
Saying come, have fun, it won't be for me.

I don't do networking, or pressing the flesh,
Here with my family is what I love best.
Perhaps if I'd done it and did play that game,
I'd have been an insider, with contacts and names.

Folk in high places, doing favours for me,
But why sell your soul, when sunsets are free?
What is the point of talking hot air?
It seems a bit desperate, that's why I'm not there.
At the end of the day, I prefer dignity,
So all that I need is my family.

If I could

If I could love you forever,
If I could love you every day,
If I could take your hand, would you understand
And let me show you the way?
If we could dance this dance forever,
If we could laugh without a word,
If I give you my life, will you be my wife,
Or is that too absurd?
But oh, we could have a lark, a lark,
Picnicking in the park, the park.
On Saturday night, if you feel all right,
We'll go to the pictures when it's dark.
If I were a plumber, would you love me?
If you were a waitress, I'd love you.
Could you picture us on a Number Nine bus?
To Canning Town we two, just me and you.
Yes, we could walk our ways together,
Or we could raise a family.
When I come home from work, I'll change me shirt,
And we'll sit by the fireside for tea,
Just you and me.

CANNING TOWN

Be happy

The sun came out today, did you notice?
Through the tears you cried, did you notice?
The birds were singing in the summer breeze,
The flowers were visited by the honey bees;
The smell of summer filled the air,
Did you notice that, did you even care?

You say it's a black day, with your eyes filled with tears;
But just look around you at everything here.
It's a wonderful place, why don't you see?
In the garden of England, beneath the oak tree,
You could count your blessings, instead of your tears,
You could give me a smile and forget all your fears.

Let's walk through the meadow and down to the stream,
Where the swans pass us by, so regal, serene.
Live for today, live life, have fun,
Because all too soon your tomorrows won't come.
Don't leave with regrets, live your life to the full;
Just give me a smile, be happy, that's all.

Providence

A rash of stabbings, time after time,
There in my shadow, walking behind.
A free spirit that burns, with so much to give,
An Italian child, live and let live.

All the memories remembered, from time after time,
As you walked so softly, so softly behind.
Creative and clever, gifted and bright,
Sweet mother of two and a dreamer at night.

A thinker by day, with tales to invent,
Papers not read, letters not sent.
Life in a bubble, away from the world,
Still searching and looking, a restless wild girl.

And what times we had, in a castle of our own,
The castle still stands, but the children have flown.
The sausages were pricked, we travelled so far,
As you played your licks on so many guitars.

I still love your songs, both clever and true.
And I suppose, when I remember, I still love you.

Milk and honey

I'm sitting on the Underground, underneath
    my London town,
A carriage packed, a sardine can; weird that
    I'm the Englishman,
While foreign tongues loudly wag, in clothes
    that come from old Baghdad.
Multi-cultural, one and all, have some
    jumped over the China Wall?
This is London, the place to be, from
    Canning Town to Battersea.
Every nation, colour and creed, if you cut
    me, Johnny, do I not bleed?
So many people, it makes you think;
    if more come here, we may well sink.
Drowned and sunk by a foreign weight, by
    people from another state.
It's good for Britain, yes indeed, to have so
    many mouths to feed,
To have nowhere for folks to live, amazing
    how we give and give.
Ivory-towered politicians, thank you for
    your kind permission

To let me in and keep me here; I love the
taste of English beer.
Benefits for one and all, the NHS at beck
and call,
A land of milk, a land of honey, a place for
me to make some money
To send back to my family, somewhere over
land and sea.
Excuse me mate, excuse me please, the
next stop is the one for me.

Mother nature

Listen to that thunder roar, electric fingers reach
    out to earth,
Shocking and lightening the night.
Dogs cower under kitchen tables, as cats scream
    in panic and fright.
If they only knew, it's only God, God up there
    in heaven,
Moving his furniture here and there.
Don't be worried, don't be scared;
Unless you're a golfer, or a tree in a field,
There's no need to worry, I doubt you'll be killed.
I love the thunder, it reminds me again,
Where would we be without life-giving rain?

The wind and the rain on the window pane, the
    rainbow full of hope,
The power, the glory, mountains kissing the skies,
Mysterious moon and her dancing stars, the
    soaring eagle that flies.

Wonders of the world, cloaked in your four
    seasons,

The miracle of life, blessed by early spring,
In winter all seemed dead, but now all lives again.
I hope you forgive the footprint we make,
The knives we stick in you.
Your majesty reigns in spite of mankind,
Mother nature knows no end;
Thank you, Mother, for being a friend.

Today is my birthday

Today is my birthday; hip hip hooray! Not just another
    Wednesday, but a special day.
The day that I turned up; today I arrived – thanks Mum
    and Dad for giving me life.
I am so glad I chose you and glad you chose me, to enter
    this world and join your family.
Did both of you wonder what I would become? Thanks
    again, Dad, thanks again, Mum.
Your selfless love, the sacrifice, the effort you made,
    just to make it all nice,
The bruises and cuts, the tears and the smiles, the
    freedom you gave me, mile upon mile.
Age is a number, I've heard people say; my number keeps
    rising, but that's still OK.
In my mind I'm much younger, about twenty-three.
    Strange how this birthday is older than me.
Of course when you're younger, your birthdays are big,
But as you get older, you don't give a fig.
But thanks for the cards and the fab presents, too,
At the end of the day, Mum, it was all down to you.

Wales

There is snow on the mountain, here in North Wales,
In the land of the dragon, under Milk Wood tales.
There is a welcome in the hillsides, as the miners' choirs
    sing.
In the valleys and the village, a kestrel takes wing.

A land of their fathers, Thomas and Jones,
A land of great beauty, the Welsh people's home,
Where Myfanwy was born, where Myfanwy once played,
In the streams and the farmland, in the soft, sun-kissed
    day.

The union of rugby, the pride of the team,
The sheep in the fields, the stone walls between,
The daffodils that dance in the springtime breeze,
As the lambs run and play, their sheepdogs to tease.

My favourite teacher was Welsh, Mr Lloyd;
He taught me English when I was a boy,
With big bushy eyebrows and a voice like a song,
He inspired and guided, when I got things wrong.

Perhaps in your school life you met someone like him,
A teacher that gave life to the curriculum.
He spoke English and Welsh, a mystery to me,
But I remember that panad means a nice cup of tea.
It's a wonderful country, just next to my own,
With wonderful people that call Wales home.

Imperial wizard

Free the people, don't make them wait; pity the
      people, don't make a mistake.
Let go your press men, undo your press gangs,
Hold up your head high, make one honest stand.

Because you know what they want and you're
      here for the grace of God;
You send your generals to the front; any uprising
      will succumb to your gun.

You took free speech from the people that
      spoke.
Hungary is hungry, the people are broke.
Imperial wizard, salt mine king,
What kind of state of mind must your state
      be in?

Because you know what they want and you're
      here for the grace of God,
You send your generals to the front; any
      uprising will succumb to your gun.

Too many people don't feel like they're free;
Your high ideals look the lowest to me.
Open a window, let the sun shine on in,
There's more to living than killing, killing.

Sonny Rae

A boy I know called Sonny Rae, he came home today;
With his sparkling eyes, he lit the room, little Sonny Rae.
Heaven-sent, angel boy, where will your journey end?
On land or sea, remember me, I'll always be your friend.
And if I miss your big success, enjoy it just the same,
Thank you for coming, little man, Sonny Rae by name.

You were worth the wait, you really were, your
     mummy loves you loads.
She will be there to walk with you, to walk your
     future roads.
You smile that smile, Sonny shine, dream your
     dreams away,
As we watch you grow, in a summer field, rolling
     in the hay.

Your first step, your first word, those days we
     will remember.
Your first goal, your gentle soul, snowmen in December,
Pirate, cowboy, soldier, too, by the dying camp fire ember.
Let us run your race, let us fly your flag, shining special
     one.

Tell us who you are, keep us in your heart, that beats
    just like a drum.
When you look like that, I have to say, you look
    just like your mum.

Hearts turn to stone

Feel the spirit in the sky,
Touch the mountains so high,
See the woman, see the man,
Watch them working on the land.

Watch the river roll to the sea,
Sing your song, boys,
We are free.
We're a long way from home,
Watching hearts turn into stone.

See the birds fly on the wing,
Not a sound now,
They don't sing.
Watch the faces passing by,
See the anger in their eyes,
Watching hearts turn into stone.

America

It seems to be the fashion now, to knock
    America,
Malign, dismiss, for a quick french kiss, the
    banner and the star.
A world policeman I suppose we need, so
    where would we be without
A hamburger, a nice hot dog, from the land
    of the holloa and shout?

Oh Disneyland, Mickey Mouse, Obama and
    a drone,
Brave and free, look down on me, in my
    humble home.
Americans are nice, I think, though some folk
    think they're loud,
Naive perhaps, and insular, living in a cloud;
Big of heart, generous and childlike in their
    ways,
But a valuable friend up to the end, so I
    reckon that's okay.

Americana, cinerama, Hollywood movie
treats,
Baseball and American football – you don't
play with your feet.
Jitterbug, jive and Chubby's twist came from
those distant shores.
Where would we be without R & B and those
Seven Eleven stores?

Our cousins, the American family, hip
hopping across the Atlantic sea,
Where the sky is big, the cars are too, where
a pot of gold waits for you.
From every corner of the world, the people
came
to better themselves,
To be a part of the American dream, to be
the cat that got the cream.
Life, like a movie, yes for some, immigrants –
and still they come
To the open arms of a brand new land, where
castles can be made of sand.

Stardust

Ah, look what they've done to the Rock 'n' Roll clown,
Ah, Rock 'n' Roll clown is down on the ground.
Well, he used to high fly, but he crashed out the sky;
In the stardust ring, a Rock 'n' Roll king is down.

Roll on up, won't you come and take a look at me, ah
Come on, stand in line, just one at a time, see me,
See my painted-on grin, as I stand up to sing.
In the stardust ring, a Rock 'n' Roll king is down.

But he's the leader of the band, a lonely man;
Do you want to take his hand, you know you can.
Yes, I used to fly high, but I crashed out the sky.
In the stardust ring, the Rock 'n' Roll king is down,
In the stardust ring, the Rock 'n' Roll king is down.

The sprite

Wandering through a green Celtic land,
Where dragons roar and mountains still stand,
Where Dylan and Thomas walk under Milk Wood,
Where folk from the north are not understood
By Anglo neighbours that live in the east,
Where a princess calmed a troubled beast.

Who could have known their hearts would entwine
As the snow fell so deep, in the winter of time?
Guarded and troubled, she, fearing the worst,
The beast so mighty, the love affair cursed;
To give him her heart, but at what cost?
To carry her off, lonely and lost,
Make her his own, the beast of the east,
A kind word from the princess, some compassion at least.

But destiny woke, the savage beast calmed,
Like the smile of a child, cradled safe in your arms.
Time can stand still, time can fly by,
Beauty, they say, is all in the eye,
The eye of the beholder, the eye of the soul.
She looked into his eyes, the beast bowed his head;

Always your friend, the beast gently said.
She reached for his hand and at last saw the man;
A man, not a beast and so it began,
Two hearts locked together, in a green Celtic land.

Verity

Birthday girl, my treasure, my love,
A gift from heaven, a gift from above.
A star that shines in this life of mine,
Born this very day.

My daughter, a mother now, wise and strong,
With love and beauty, you carry on.
I remember you as a babe in my arms,
Your smile, your tears, held safe from harm;
Just you and I, in Piglet's room,
As the light shone bright from that winter moon.

I knew you were special, yes I knew back then,
As you smiled in my eyes, my special friend.
Back in that winter of seventy-two,
Alone in that room, just me and you.
As a little girl growing, so pretty in pink,
So many times I stop and I think
How empty my life would be without you,
Your love and your laughter, helping me through.

Thank you for choosing me as your dad,
Thank you for all the good times we've had.
As the years pass by, my love remains strong,
Forever, my love, on and on,
Through the twists and the turns,
Through the ups and the downs,
I'll always be with you, always around,
To help to protect, to whisper to you,
This love is forever, this love is so true.
My Verity, remember me, you are the friend
To whom the shadows of far years extend.
Whether by your side or far away,
In my heart you will always stay.

Heart beats like a drum

Are we lost in time and space?
Do we know just where we're going?
Are we standing on the outside looking in?
And of all the love I've known,
There is only just your heartbeat
That moves with the rhythm of my own.

And oh, my heart beats like a drum,
Crashing like a cymbal, burning like the sun.

Did you ever think that we
Could stand so close together?
It's surprising what you can do if you try;
You understand so well, you seem to know me better,
Better than in fact I know myself.

And oh, my heart beats like a drum,
You can take it from me, our life has just begun;
Through the corridors and pathways to heaven,
    we will fly.

Dangerous

This boy is dangerous to know;
He'll steal your heart and let you go
Into the dark and cold shadows.
He'll drag you down with him below,
But you love him, yeah you love him and he loves you.
He cast a spell all over you.

You're lost and you can't see the truth;
He's gonna leave you black and blue.
This boy is danger, through and through,
But you love him, yes you love him and he loves you.
Dangerous, so dangerous, he's dangerous,
Girl, for you, yes girl, for you.

I know you're caught up in a web of lies.
You never see the truth inside his eyes.
Just like a puppet on a string,
He calls the tune; you dance and sing.
But you love him, yes, you love him and he loves you.
He loves you.
Dangerous, he's so dangerous,
Dangerous, this boy is dangerous.

Sweet dreams

Sleep, like a velvet corridor, where dreams unlock a
    subconscious door,
Where the impossible is possible and unlikely scenes
    are played.
Real but yet untouchable, they live and then may fade,
Fading in the morning's light, forgotten, lost and
    out of sight;
Lost in the darkness, in the quiet cloak of night.
In a dream I flew over China, with rickshaws far below,
Kissed Doris Day too, on the lips, but that was a
    while ago.
Running fast and running, but getting to nowhere;
But as heavy as we sleep, dreamer, be aware,
Of the twists, the turns that burn inside,
The nightmare's ghostly stare,
As it carries us off to its world below,
To a dark and shadowy place unknown.
Awful and terrible, real and surreal
Collide in black shadows, our sweet dreams to steal.

All together

Outside the rain is falling, inside the fire's warm,
And here we are now, all together.
The road was filled with glory,
We wrote that awesome story,
Now don't it feel good to be together,
And as our spirits fly, into the rain-filled sky,
We say a prayer. Are you there?

I know that I'll remember this dark day in December,
When we were all here, all together.
By train and car and plane, we made it all the same,
Now look at us here, here together.

I catch your smiling eyes, we laugh until we cry;
What a day, what a time,
And as our spirits fly, into the rain-filled sky,
We say a prayer. Are you there?
Don't it feel good together, all of us here together,
Everybody's home.

At the end of the day

At the end of the day, I hear you say,
    when all is said and done,
Reasons and rhymes, lines that rhyme,
    I hope that it's been fun.
And if this book made you smile, or even
    made you think,
I appreciate you taking a look, with a smile
    and a knowing wink.
A nod to the past, a thought or two,
    an opinion here and there.
Thank you, friend, for taking a look.
    It's good to know you care.
Over and out, till next we meet, good health
    and happiness.
May the road you travel bring luck and love;
    I wish you the very best.